"BRING THE CLASSICS TO LIFE"

Oliver Twist

LEVEL 3

Series Designer
Philip J. Solimene

Editor
Laura Solimene

EDCON
Long Island, New York

Story Adaptor
Lewann Sotnak

Author
Charles Dickens

About the Author

Charles Dickens was born in England in the year 1812. As a boy, he spent a lot of time reading books. When Charles finished school he became a newspaper reporter. Later, he wrote many books of his own. Some of his most famous were *David Copperfield, A Christmas Carol, Great Expectations, A Tale of Two Cities,* and *Oliver Twist.*

Copyright © 1998
A/V Concepts Corp.
Long Island, New York

Printed in U.S.A.
ISBN # 1-55576-325-1

CONTENTS

Words Used 4, 5

WORDS USED

Story 71	Story 72	Story 73	Story 74	Story 75
KEY WORDS				
astonish	age	dirt	brush	against
bowl	beg	half	healthy	husband
doctor	cellar	judge	laid	lying
pleasant	downstairs	several	pillow	planned
spoon	lazy	sparkle	tight	rich
sweep	paid	thief	wipe	we're
NECESSARY WORDS				
born	beat	awake	God	gun
cereal	funeral	blood		information
charge	sir	bookstore		niece
dead		court		reward
die		handkerchief		robbery
job		knife		servant
owner		officer		shot
		pocketbook		
		rob/robbed		

WORDS USED

Story 76	Story 77	Story 78	Story 79	Story 80
KEY WORDS				
beyond	became	eleven	drag	alike
company	become	helping	hid	America
depend	below	hug	often	child
disappoint	famous	meet	spare	daughter
doesn't	flow	steal	spot	earn
shadow	mind	though	struck	history
NECESSARY WORDS				
alive	buggy	danger	hate	adopt
church	inn	midnight	murder	forgiven
learned	locket	Sunday		minister
rent	meanwhile	warn		mistake
son				prison

Young Oliver

PREPARATION

Key Words

astonish	(əs ton´ish)	surprise greatly *I will <u>astonish</u> Mother by cleaning my room.*
bowl	(bōl)	a hollow, round dish *I had a <u>bowl</u> of soup for dinner.*
doctor	(dok´tər)	someone who helps people who are hurt or not well *Mother took me to see a <u>doctor</u> when I broke my arm.*
pleasant	(plez´nt)	anything or anyone that pleases 1. *We had a <u>pleasant</u> day at the beach.* 2. *Our neighbors are <u>pleasant</u> people.*
spoon	(spün)	something you use for eating or dishing up food *I eat soup with a <u>spoon</u>.*
sweep	(swēp)	to brush away dirt *"Will you <u>sweep</u> the floor for me?" asked Mother.*

Young Oliver

Necessary Words

born	(bôrn)	brought forth; come into the world *My baby brother was <u>born</u> today.*
cereal	(sir´ ē əl)	food made from grain such as rice, corn, oats or barley *Today I had <u>cereal</u> for breakfast.*
charge	(chärj)	1. to rule over with care *Pete's in <u>charge</u> of the money.* 2. care *Mary has <u>charge</u> of her brother when her mother is away.*
dead	(ded)	something that has no life in it *The tree's <u>dead</u> leaves were falling.*
die	(dī)	to stop living *Plants will <u>die</u> if they get no water.*
job	(job)	work done for money *My sister found a <u>job</u> today.*
owner	(ōn´ər)	a person who has (owns) a thing *I'm the <u>owner</u> of a new car.*

Places

England   is the largest part of Great Britain.

Things

chimney sweep   is a person who cleans the inside of chimneys.

Young Oliver

Oliver is born. But he will never get to know his mother.

Preview:
1. Read the name of the story.
2. Look at the picture.
3. Read the sentences under the picture.
4. Read the first three paragraphs of the story.
5. Then answer the following question.

You learned from your preview that people who lived in a workhouse were
____a. sick.
____b. young.
____c. poor.
____d. happy.

Turn to the Comprehension Check on page 10 for the right answer.

Now read the story.

Read to find out about young Oliver's hard life.

Young Oliver

Long ago in England there was a workhouse in most every town. Poor people, who had no place to go, lived in a workhouse. But they did not live for *free*. That's why it was called a workhouse. They would eat and sleep at the workhouse. But they went to work outside the workhouse. The little money they made went to the workhouse to help pay for their food. And when children were old enough, they went to work, too!

One night at the workhouse, Oliver Twist was born. His mother sat up. "Let me see my baby, then I will die," she said.

"Oh, you must not talk about wanting to die," said the doctor. But Oliver's mother patted her baby, then fell back and died.

"Too bad," said the doctor. "Who was she, anyway?"

"No one knows," the doctor's helper answered. "She fell in the street outside. Her baby was ready to be born. We do not know her name, or where she came from."

Little Oliver's early years were hard. He and the other children at the workhouse had little to eat. Mrs. Mann, the woman in charge, was mean to the children. She hit them often...and liked doing it! And she took the children's food money to spend on herself! So little Oliver went hungry most of the time.

Sometimes Mr. Bumble came to see the children. It was his job to see that the children were being cared for. It was his job to tell the owners how the children were doing. But like Mrs. Mann, he did not like children. So he didn't do his job real well.

"How are the children getting along?" he asked Mrs. Mann, one day.

"Oh, the children are so dear," Mrs. Mann said, in a pleasant way. "I love them all so much."

Mr. Bumble just looked around and smiled. He never talked with the children to see how they were *really* doing. He was happy just to hear a good word. Then he could hurry out of there. But as soon as he would leave, Mrs. Mann would put on her mean face again.

For many years, Oliver worked hard at the workhouse. His friends worked hard, too. They boys had little time for fun and games. And all their hard work made them *very* hungry. But all they were given was a little cooked cereal to eat. The boys would eat all the cereal in their bowls. But always, the boys were hungry and wanted more. One day the boys told Oliver, "You go ask for some more cereal."

Oliver took his bowl and spoon and went to the cook. "Please, I would like some more," he said.

The cook got very angry. "You astonish me!" he said. "It is a *terrible* thing to ask for more of *anything*!" He picked up a big, long spoon and hit Oliver with it. Then he shouted for Mr. Bumble.

Mr. Bumble came running into the kitchen. He was astonished at the terrible thing Oliver had asked of the cook. Mr. Bumble ran to tell the owners.

"Oliver has asked for more cereal," Mr. Bumble told the owners.

"*What?*" said one of the men, as he brought his hand down and hit the table. "He *knows* he should not have asked for more. He already *had* his cereal!" The man was not at all pleasant. Mr. Bumble became a little frightened.

Mr. Bumble locked Oliver in a dark room all alone. Every other day he took Oliver into the room where the other boys ate. In front of the boys, he hit Oliver again and again. This was to let the boys know they must not ask for more of *anything!*

One day Mr. Bumble put a sign outside on the gate: *BOY LOOKING FOR WORK.* Mr. Bumble wanted to get Oliver out of his hair. And a job outside would do just that!

First, a chimney sweep stopped in. He wanted Oliver to sweep the inside of chimneys. This man did not care about the boys who worked for him. Sometimes, he let them burn in the chimneys. But the men at the workhouse would not let Oliver sweep chimneys. So Mr. Bumble put another sign outside: *HARD-WORKING BOY LOOKING FOR WORK.*

This time, Mr. Sowerberry saw the sign. He made boxes to hold dead people. He needed someone to help him in his shop. So he took Oliver with him to live and work.

At his new home, Mrs. Sowerberry looked Oliver over. She was not a pleasant woman. "He's *very* small for his nine years," she said to Mr. Sowerberry.

"But he will grow, my dear," he answered.

"Yes, he will," Mrs. Sowerberry said, in a cross voice. "He'll grow on *our* food and drink! Come here, Oliver, you little bag of bones. You can have the pieces of food we give our dog."

Oliver was so hungry that he ate every last bite. Mrs. Sowerberry's face looked more cross than before. *This boy will eat us right into the poor house*, she thought to herself.

Mrs. Sowerberry took Oliver next door to Mr. Sowerberry's shop. "You can sleep by the boxes we use for dead people," she said. And smiling, she left the shop.

Oliver looked around the shop. He was afraid. And he felt so alone. Little Oliver sat down and cried himself to sleep.

Young Oliver

COMPREHENSION CHECK

Choose the best answer.

1. Oliver's mother died when Oliver
   _____a. was three years' old.
   _____b. was two days' old.
   _____c. went to work.
   _____d. was born.

2. The people who ran the workhouse
   _____a. were kind to the children.
   _____b. were mean to the children.
   _____c. never hit the children.
   _____d. made the children happy.

3. Why were the boys at the workhouse always hungry?
   _____a. Mrs. Mann was spending the food money on herself.
   _____b. Mr. Bumble was taking all the food money.
   _____c. The owners were taking all the food money.
   _____d. They wouldn't eat the cook's food.

4. Growing up in the workhouse
   _____a. was fun for the boys.
   _____b. was hard on the boys.
   _____c. would make the boys strong.
   _____d. made the boys feel lucky.

5. It was Mr. Bumble's job
   _____a. to keep the owners happy.
   _____b. to put the children to work.
   _____c. to see that the children were being cared for.
   _____d. to do the food shopping.

6. Oliver got into trouble when he
   _____a. told the cook to take a day off.
   _____b. asked the cook for a second helping.
   _____c. asked Mrs. Mann if he could play a game.
   _____d. had a fight with another boy.

7. First, Oliver asked the cook for some more cereal. Then, the cook shouted for Mr. Bumble. Next,
   _____a. Mr. Bumble locked Oliver in a dark room.
   _____b. Mr. Bumble hit Oliver.
   _____c. Oliver was sent to live with the Sowerberrys.
   _____d. Mr. Bumble ran to tell the owners what Oliver had done.

8. Oliver felt afraid and all alone at the Sowerberrys. He missed
   _____a. Mrs. Mann.
   _____b. Mr. Bumble.
   _____c. his friends.
   _____d. his mother.

9. Another name for this story could be
   _____a. "More, Please."
   _____b. "Growing Up in a Workhouse."
   _____c. "A Little Bag of Bones."
   _____d. "Off to Work."

10. This story is mainly about
   _____a. how the poor people of England lived.
   _____b. a young boy growing up without his family.
   _____c. a young boy who never got enough to eat.
   _____d. a nine-year-old boy who got a job.

Check your answers with the key on page 67.

Young Oliver

VOCABULARY CHECK

astonish	bowl	doctor	pleasant	spoon	sweep

I. Sentences to Finish
Fill in the blank in each sentence with the correct key word from the box above.

1. "Call a _____. I think my nose is broken!"

2. I like Barbara. She's a very _____person.

3. I set the table with a knife, a fork, and a _____.

4. I will _____Linda when I ask her to marry me.

5. My sister said, "It's your turn to _____ the floor.

6. I ate a big _____of ice cream for dessert.

II. Word Search
All the words from the box above are hidden in the puzzle below. They may be written from left to right, or up and down. As you find each word, put a circle around it. One word, that is not a key word, has been done for you.

```
P  L  E  I (P  L  A  Y) A
A  B  O  W  L  O  W  A  S
S  W  S  W  E  E  P  S  T
T  O  P  D  A  W  B  T  O
O  O  L  O  S  P  O  O  N
N  A  E  C  A  A  W  N  S
S  Y  A  O  N  S  X  I  W
W  D  O  C  T  O  R  S  E
E  B  P  L  E  A  S  H  P
```

Check your answers with the key on page 69.

This page may be reproduced for classroom use.

Oliver Runs Away

PREPARATION

Key Words

age	(āj)	time of life; the length of life *What is the <u>age</u> of your brother?*
beg	(beg)	to ask for something *The man in the street will often <u>beg</u> for money.*
cellar	(sel´ər)	a room, or rooms, under the floor of a building *Long ago, people kept food in the <u>cellar</u>.*
downstairs	(doun´stãrz´)	the room, or rooms, that are down the stairs *Mother told us to go <u>downstairs</u> to play.*
lazy	(lā´zē)	1. not willing to work *The <u>lazy</u> man would not look for a job.* 2. moving slowly *We spent a <u>lazy</u> day at the beach.*
paid	(pād)	given money for work *I was <u>paid</u> ten dollars to rake the leaves.*

Oliver Runs Away

Necessary Words

beat   (bēt)   to hit over and over
The angry man <u>beat</u> his dog.

funeral   (fū´nər əl)   a time when people get together to remember someone who has died
Grandmother's <u>funeral</u> was a sad time for all of us.

sir   (sėr)   a word we say when talking to an important person
"Yes, <u>sir</u>, I will do as you ask."

Places

London   is a big city in England.

13

Oliver Runs Away

Oliver wakes up to the sound of someone kicking at the door.

Preview: 1. Read the name of the story.
2. Look at the picture.
3. Read the sentence under the picture.
4. Read the first five paragraphs of the story.
5. Then answer the following question.

You learned from your preview that Noah Claypole was

____a. a mean, young boy.
____b. a kind, young man.
____c. a hard-working boy.
____d. lazy.

Turn to the Comprehension Check on page 16 for the right answer.

Now read the story.

Read to find out about why Oliver ran away.

Oliver Runs Away

Oliver had fallen asleep in Mr. Sowerberry's shop. But he did not sleep well that night. He woke up many times, wishing he was dead.

In the morning, Oliver woke to a kicking noise at the door. "Open the door, lazy boy!" someone shouted.

Oliver got up and opened the door. An older boy stood there, looking very angry. "Do you know who I am, Workhouse Boy?" he asked Oliver.

"No, sir. But if you need a box for someone who has died, I can help you," Oliver answered.

"I don't need no box!" shouted the boy. "I'm Noah Claypole, and I'm in charge of you. Take the covers off these windows, lazy boy, *right now!*" Then Noah gave Oliver a kick in the leg.

For many years, children had made fun of Noah. They were very mean to him. They laughed at him because his mother and father were poor. But at least he *had* a mother and father. Oliver did not. This made Noah feel that he was better than Oliver. Now it was Noah's turn to be mean to someone else.

Oliver was not happy living with the Sowerberrys. And he did not think much of Noah Claypole. He did his work, but he didn't like it.

"Look at his sad face," said Mrs. Sowerberry, one day. "Why, Oliver would be a good one to look sad at a funeral."

"Why, that's a *great* idea!" said Mr. Sowerberry. "I might get paid more money if I have someone to look sad at my funerals." So part of Oliver's job was to look sad at every funeral.

The idea had worked! Mr. Sowerberry was making more money than ever. And Mr. Sowerberry was pleased with Oliver's work. Sometimes he paid Oliver a little money. When Noah found out about this, he got real angry. *Why should Oliver have it better than me?* he

thought to himself. *He's not going to get away with this!*

One day Noah asked Oliver, "What happened to your mother, Workhouse Boy?"

"She died, sir," Oliver said, sadly.

"Well," said Noah, "that's too bad. I bet she died because she was a bad woman." Noah cracked a smile. He couldn't wait to see little Oliver cry.

"Don't you *ever* say anything bad about my mother!" shouted Oliver. He took hold of Noah's neck and shook him silly. Then he hit Noah so hard, that the bigger boy fell to the floor.

"Help! Help!" shouted Noah. "Oliver is trying to kill me!"

Mrs. Sowerberry came running when she heard Noah's cries for help. Seeing Noah on the floor, she didn't ask what had happened. She took Oliver by the hair and began to beat him. But Oliver had had enough! He began to beat back. They hit each other over and over, while Noah did nothing. Then, with one, big push, Mrs. Sowerberry threw Oliver downstairs. He landed in the cellar.

Noah ran to the workhouse. "Come quick, Mr. Bumble! Oliver is trying to kill us all. And Mr. Sowerberry isn't home!"

Mr. Bumble ran back to the house with Noah. Mrs. Sowerberry told him what Oliver had done. "He beat up Noah, and then he came at me," she said. "Why, if I hadn't pushed him downstairs, we might both be dead!"

Mr. Bumble went downstairs to the cellar. He picked Oliver up by the ear and began to beat him. Between blows, Oliver tried to tell him what had *really* happened. But Mr. Bumble would not listen. When the beating was over, Oliver was sent to bed. For supper, Mrs. Sowerberry brought him some bread and water.

That's it! Oliver said to himself. *I've had enough! When the sun comes up, I'm out of here!*

At first light, Oliver got his few clothes. He took the little money he had saved, and the bread left over from supper. He quietly left the shop and ran and ran. *I'll go to London,* he thought. *No one will find me there!*

For two nights, Oliver fell asleep in the grass. Soon, his bread and money were gone. He tried to beg for food, but the people chased him away from their homes. Dogs chased him away from their farms. He did not eat for many days. But he was never going back to the workhouse. He was not going back to the Sowerberrys'.

As he sat on some steps thinking of what to do, a boy walked up to him. "My name is Jack Dawkins," he said. "You don't look well, are you sick or something?"

"No, I'm not sick," answered Oliver. "I'm just hungry. I haven't eaten in many days. I've tried begging, but I haven't had any luck."

Jack bought Oliver something to eat. "Why don't you come with me to London?" he asked Oliver. "I know of a place where you will get food and a bed. You won't have to beg. Fagin, the man in charge, will take good care of you. You will even get paid sometimes."

Oliver went with Jack to London. They went to a house on a terrible street. The houses were dirty and falling to pieces. *This place doesn't look too good,* Oliver thought to himself. He thought of running away again, but Jack had him by the hand.

Inside the house, Oliver saw many boys his age. "This is my new friend, Oliver Twist," Jack told Fagin and the boys.

Oliver's thoughts of running away were soon put to rest. Fagin gave Oliver the best supper he had eaten in a long time. And his new bed was better than the hard ground he had been sleeping on.

Oliver Runs Away

COMPREHENSION CHECK

Choose the best answer.

1. Why do you think Oliver wished he was dead?
   _____a. He missed his mother.
   _____b. He didn't like the Sowerberrys.
   _____c. He thought his life would never get better.
   _____d. He didn't sleep well.

2. First, Oliver woke up to the sound of someone kicking at the door. Then, Oliver answered the door. Next,
   _____a. Noah pulled the covers off the windows.
   _____b. Oliver made fun of Noah.
   _____c. Oliver hit Noah for waking him up.
   _____d. Noah kicked Oliver in the leg.

3. Noah was mean to everyone because
   _____a. he was just like his father.
   _____b. the Sowerberrys made him this way.
   _____c. no one had ever been kind to him.
   _____d. that was his job.

4. Oliver's sad face
   _____a. got him a job working at funerals.
   _____b. made everyone unhappy.
   _____c. made people feel sorry for him.
   _____d. pleased Mrs. Sowerberry.

5. What did Oliver do that made Noah real mad?
   _____a. He made the Sowerberrys happy.
   _____b. He was paid money to do an easy job.
   _____c. He moved into the Sowerberrys' house.
   _____d. He took Saturdays off.

6. When Noah talked bad about Oliver's mother,
   _____a. Noah got what was coming to him.
   _____b. Oliver just stood there and took it.
   _____c. Oliver laughed it off.
   _____d. Oliver started to cry.

7. Who pushed Oliver downstairs and into the cellar?
   _____a. Noah
   _____b. Mr. Bumble
   _____c. Mr. Sowerberry
   _____d. Mrs. Sowerberry

8. When Oliver ran away, he
   _____a. lived in the streets.
   _____b. found a lot of people to help him.
   _____c. made lots of friends.
   _____d. never went hungry.

9. Another name for this story could be
   _____a. "Oliver Goes to London."
   _____b. "Working Hard."
   _____c. "A Friend Named Noah."
   _____d. "The Funeral."

10. This story is mainly about
   _____a. a boy who runs away from the mean people he lives with.
   _____b. a boy who goes looking for his family.
   _____c. Oliver's new friend, Jack Dawkins.
   _____d. why the Sowerberrys did not like Oliver.

Check your answers with the key on page 67.

This page may be reproduced for classroom use.

Oliver Runs Away

VOCABULARY CHECK

age	beg	cellar	downstairs	lazy	paid

I. Sentences to Finish
Fill in the blank in each sentence with the correct key word from the box above.

1. My grandfather died at a very young _____.

2. Mrs. Fox _____ me twenty dollars to cut the grass.

3. I feel _____ today. I think I'll stay in bed.

4. Let's go _____ and watch T.V.

5. If I _____ Mother, she might let me go to the party.

6. It is cold and wet down in the _____.

II. Matching
Write the letter of the correct meaning from Column B next to the key word in Column A.

Column A	Column B
_____1. age	a. not willing to work
_____2. paid	b. to ask for something
_____3. downstairs	c. time of life; the length of life
_____4. beg	d. given money for work
_____5. cellar	e. the room, or rooms that are down the stairs
_____6. lazy	f. a room, or rooms, under the floor of a building

Check your answers with the key on page 69.

Fagin's Game

PREPARATION

Key Words

dirt	(dėrt)	1. loose soil or earth *The heavy rains turned the <u>dirt</u> into mud.* 2. mud, soil, or anything that makes something unclean *"Go wash the <u>dirt</u> off your face," said Mom.*
half	(haf)	one of two equal parts *<u>Half</u> of four is two.*
judge	(juj)	someone who hears and decides cases in court *The <u>judge</u> sent the robber to jail.*
several	(sev´ ər əl)	more than two or three of something *It took <u>several</u> hours to clean the house.*
sparkle	(spär´kl)	shine *Katy's eyes seemed to <u>sparkle</u> when we told her the good news.*
thief	(thēf)	someone who takes something that doesn't belong to him or her *The policeman caught the <u>thief</u> who took my car.*
rob **robbed**	(rob)	to take something that is not yours; steal 1. *The man planned to <u>rob</u> the store.* 2. *I was <u>robbed</u> last night.*

Fagin's Game

Necessary Words

awake (ə wāk´) not asleep
The storm kept me <u>awake</u> all night.

blood (blud) the red liquid found in the veins
Your heart sends <u>blood</u> to all the parts of your body.

bookstore (bŭk´stôr´) a store where books are sold
The <u>bookstore</u> is not open today.

court (kôrt) a room or building where matters of law are decided by a judge
I must be in <u>court</u> at two o'clock.

handkerchief (hang´ kər chif) a soft, square of cloth used to wipe the nose, face, or other parts
Pete put a clean <u>handkerchief</u> in his pocket.

knife (nīf) a sharp tool used for cutting
I used a <u>knife</u> to cut the rope.

officer (ôf ´ə sər) someone who holds a public or government office, such as a police officer or court officer
My brother is a police <u>officer</u>.

pocketbook (pok´it bŭk´) a case used for carrying money and other things
Mother can't find her <u>pocketbook</u>.

Fagin's Game

Fagin, thinking that Oliver is asleep, gets out his secret box.

Preview:
1. Read the name of the story.
2. Look at the picture.
3. Read the sentence under the picture.
4. Read the first paragraph of the story.
5. Then answer the following question.

You learned from your preview that Fagin kept many things in a secret place
____a. in the cellar.
____b. under the floor.
____c. under Oliver's bed.
____d. in the kitchen.

Turn to the Comprehension Check on page 22 for the right answer.

Now read the story.

Read to find out how Oliver gets into more trouble.

Fagin's Game

The sun was just beginning to come up. Oliver turned over in his bed. As he rolled over, he saw Fagin in the room. With eyes half-closed, he saw Fagin take a box from under a board in the floor. Fagin held up several things. The first was a beautiful, gold watch. Oliver saw it sparkle in the sun's light. Then Fagin took out several gold rings with stones that sparkled. Just then, Fagin saw that Oliver's eyes were half-open. He quickly put the things back into the box.

"Are you awake, Boy?" asked Fagin. He pulled a knife from his pocket. He shook the knife at Oliver. "Did you see my pretty things?" he asked.

"Yes, sir. I saw several things," answered Oliver, in a whisper. He was frightened by Fagin's knife.

Fagin's eyes grew wide. "How long have you been awake?" he asked.

The look in Fagin's eyes gave Oliver goose bumps. He didn't know what to say.

"*Speak up, Boy!*" Fagin roared. "*Quickly - if you want to stay alive!*"

Oliver was very much awake now. "I just woke up now," he said. "I'm sorry if I made you cross."

Fagin put the knife away. "Ah, I was just trying to frighten you," Fagin lied. "But don't ever let me catch you getting into my things. They are all I have to live on in my old age." Then he put the box away.

"Yes, sir, I won't go near your things," said Oliver. "May I get up now?" Oliver knew that Fagin did not wish to talk about the things in the box.

"You can wash off your dirt in that bowl in the corner," said Fagin. "Then we will have breakfast."

Just then, Jack Dawkins came in with Charley Bates.

Fagin looked at the two boys. "Have you boys been hard at work this morning?"

"Hard as nails," answered Jack.

Fagin smiled. "Good boys. So, what have you brought me this morning?"

The boys held out two pocket-books, one handkerchief, then several shiny things. Fagin put the shiny things away. He turned to Oliver. "These pocketbooks and handkerchiefs are all well-made, don't ya think?"

"Yes, sir, they are very fine," said Oliver.

Fagin put his arm around Oliver. "Come, Oliver," he said. "We will play a game. We will teach you about our work."

Fagin put the handkerchief, a watch, and several other things in his pockets. Then he made believe he was looking in a shop window. The boys took turns trying to take things out of his pockets. It was important that Fagin not feel anything. If Fagin felt a hand in his pocket, he cried out. Then the game would start over.

Oliver watched the boys play Fagin's game. It looked like a silly game to him.

"Come, Oliver," said Fagin, "let the boys teach you how to play. Then someday, you will be a great man."

Oliver wondered how taking things out of pockets could make him great.

One day Fagin let Oliver go with Jack and Charley. They passed an apple stand. Jack and Charley took several apples from the stand and put them in their pockets. Then they pointed to a fine-looking man standing by the bookstore. He was reading a sign in the store's window.

Quietly, Charley and Jack picked a handkerchief out of the man's pocket. Then they ran. Oliver began to run, too, but the man shouted, "Stop, Thief!"

A man in the bookstore came running out. He ran after Oliver and caught him. He knocked him to the ground and beat him. He pulled Oliver by the arm and brought him back to the bookstore. He brought him to Mr. Brownlow, the man who had been robbed.

"Here is the thief, Mr. Brownlow. I caught him trying to run away."

Oliver was covered with dirt and blood. A policeman came by and took hold of Oliver.

"I didn't do it, sir," said Oliver. "It was two other boys."

"*Sure* it was," the policeman said. "You're coming with me to the station. You can tell it to the judge." He took hold of Oliver's hair and pulled him along.

Mr. Brownlow went along to the station. "Be careful with him," he said to the policeman. "This boy does not look like a thief."

In court the judge asked Oliver question after question. Oliver was so frightened that he fell to the floor. His eyes were half-shut.

Mr. Brownlow ran to Oliver. "This boy is not well," he told the judge.

"This boy is just making-believe," said the judge, in an angry voice. "There's nothing wrong with him." The judge looked over at one of the court's officers. "Now lock him up!"

"Stop!" cried Mr. Brownlow. "I don't believe that you have your thief. *Please* let me take the boy home," he begged. "Let me have charge of him."

So Oliver went to Mr. Brownlow's home. The kind man carefully washed Oliver. He washed away the dirt and blood. Then he put Oliver to bed.

Oliver couldn't thank Mr. Brownlow enough for what he had done. He was happy that someone believed his story. And tonight, Oliver would sleep in a soft, warm bed.

Fagin's Game

COMPREHENSION CHECK

Choose the best answer.

1. When Fagin saw Oliver's eyes half-open, he
   _____a. quietly left the room.
   _____b. pulled a knife from his pocket.
   _____c. pointed a gun to Oliver's head.
   _____d. kicked Oliver out of bed.

2. The things that Fagin had in the box
   _____a. did not really belong to him.
   _____b. had once belonged to his mother.
   _____c. belonged to Jack Dawkins.
   _____d. belonged to Charley Bates.

3. What "work" did Jack and Charley do for Fagin?
   _____a. They stole things for him.
   _____b. They cooked for him.
   _____c. They cleaned for him.
   _____d. It was their job to make the beds.

4. Fagin's "game" was
   _____a. a way to have fun indoors.
   _____b. a way to make Oliver feel at home.
   _____c. a way of teaching the boys to be great men.
   _____d. a way of teaching the boys how to steal.

5. Oliver
   _____a. liked Fagin's silly game.
   _____b. was good at Fagin's game.
   _____c. did not know what Fagin and the boys were up to.
   _____d. always got caught with his hands in Fagin's pocket.

6. Why did Oliver get caught and not the other boys?
   _____a. It was Oliver who took the man's handkerchief.
   _____b. The other boys had run away.
   _____c. Oliver had the look of a thief.
   _____d. Oliver gave himself up.

7. In court, Oliver became so frightened that
   _____a. he threw up his breakfast.
   _____b. he started to cry.
   _____c. he fell to the floor.
   _____d. he told the judge he did it.

8. The judge placed Oliver in the care of
   _____a. Mr. Bumble.
   _____b. Mr. Brownlow.
   _____c. Fagin.
   _____d. Mr. Sowerberry.

9. Another name for this story could be
   _____a. "Growing Up."
   _____b. "The Pick-Pockets."
   _____c. "A Day In Court."
   _____d. "Fagin's Joke."

10. This story is mainly about
    _____a. how Fagin got along with the young boys.
    _____b. Oliver's day in court.
    _____c. a good boy who was always getting into trouble.
    _____d. a mean judge who didn't like little boys.

Check your answers with the key on page 67.

Fagin's Game

VOCABULARY CHECK

dirt	half	judge	several	sparkle	thief

I. Sentences to Finish

Fill in the blank in each sentence with the correct key word from the box above.

1. The _____didn't know which man was telling the truth.

2. The snow seemed to _____in the sun's light.

3. The _____was sent to jail for taking the money.

4. Kim ate _____of the ice cream. Her brother ate the other _____.

5. Mike fell off his bike and landed in the _____.

6. It took _____hours to find the missing boy.

II. Word Use

Put a check next to YES if the sentence makes sense. Put a check next to NO if the sentence does not make sense.

1. *I ate **half** the cake and it was all gone!* _____YES _____NO

2. *Mom's ring seems to **sparkle** in the dark.* _____YES _____NO

3. *The **judge** did not want to send the boy to jail.* _____YES _____NO

4. *Heavy rains made the **dirt** look clean.* _____YES _____NO

5. *The **thief** never took what didn't belong to him.* _____YES _____NO

6. *It takes Mother **several** hours to shop for new clothes.* _____YES _____NO

Check your answers with the key on page 69.

This page may be reproduced for classroom use.

More Trouble For Oliver

PREPARATION

Key Words

brush	(brush)	remove or wipe away *Tim used a handkerchief to <u>brush</u> away his tears.*
healthy	(hel´thē)	feeling well; not sick *Eating the right foods keeps one <u>healthy</u>.*
laid	(lād)	put down; lay down *I <u>laid</u> my keys on the table.*
pillow	(pil´ō)	a bag or case filled with soft material *Helen and Linda had a <u>pillow</u> fight.*
tight	(tīt)	firmly *The fast ride frightened Kevin, but he held on <u>tight</u>.*
wipe	(wīp)	to take (away, off, or out) by rubbing *Sheila cried, then took a handkerchief to <u>wipe</u> her eyes.*

More Trouble For Oliver

Necessary Words

God   (god)   is a great being that many people believe in
My mother says that <u>God</u> loves everyone.

More Trouble For Oliver

Mrs. Bedwin takes good care of little Oliver.

Preview: 1. Read the name of the story.
2. Look at the picture.
3. Read the sentence under the picture.
4. Read the first two paragraphs of the story.
5. Then answer the following question.

You learned from your preview that Oliver had been sick for
____a. several days.
____b. one day.
____c. one week.
____d. several hours.

Turn to the Comprehension Check on page 28 for the right answer.

Now read the story.

Read to find out how Oliver found himself back at Fagin's place.

More Trouble For Oliver

The beating Oliver got from the man at the bookstore left him feeling very sick. For several days, he did not know if it was night or day. All he wanted to do was sleep. At last, half-awake, he asked, "Where am I?"

"You really must rest, Dear," said Mrs. Bedwin. She was the kind, old lady who kept house for Mr. Brownlow. "We don't want you getting sick again." She patted Oliver's head and pillow. His head still felt a little warm. She reached up to brush the hair from his eyes. Then she took a wet cloth to wipe his face.

Oliver reached for her hand. He held her hand tight and laid it on his neck. Mrs. Bedwin's eyes began to fill up. She took a handkerchief to wipe them. "You are such a dear boy," she told Oliver.

Soon, a doctor came to look in on Oliver. "Watch over him with great care," he told Mrs. Bedwin. "He still isn't looking very healthy. And he is not very strong."

Each day Mrs. Bedwin brought Oliver his food. She spent a lot of time cooking for him. She wanted to see him healthy again. When Oliver was finished eating, Mrs. Bedwin and Mr. Brownlow took turns reading to him.

Before long, Oliver was up and around again. He began to do more and more every day. Sometimes he just walked about the house. He liked this house very much. It was such a clean house....not at all what he was used to. Sometimes he spent his time looking at Mr. Brownlow's books. He had so many of them! *Someday I will read all the books in this house*, thought Oliver.

But Oliver spent more time looking at something else. Mr. Brownlow had many fine paintings in his house. But there was one painting that always caught Oliver's eye. It was a picture of a very beautiful woman. It hung on the wall in the library, just above the fireplace. Oliver could never walk past this picture without stopping to take a good look. As he looked at the woman in the painting, he felt very strange. He felt like the woman was alive...that she was looking right at him. He wondered who the woman in the painting could be.

One day Mr. Brownlow's good friend stopped by. His name was Mr. Grimwig. The two men talked until there was a knock at the door. It was a young lady from the bookstore. She had brought some books for Mr. Brownlow. When she saw that Mr. Brownlow had a visitor, she went away quickly. "Why didn't she wait to get paid for these books?" said Mr. Brownlow.

Oliver, feeling much better, had heard Mr. Brownlow's question. "Sir," said Oliver, "I will take the money to the bookstore for you."

"Why, thank you, Oliver. That will be a big help to me." He took some money out of his pocket and gave it to Oliver. Mr. Grimwig said nothing, but he made a face.

"Be careful, Oliver," said Mrs. Bedwin. "Hurry back before it gets dark." She wiped her eyes as she watched Oliver walk down the street. *Such a nice boy*, she thought.

Mr. Grimwig brushed the back of his head with his hand. "How can you believe that boy?" he asked Mr. Brownlow. "I bet he never makes it to the bookstore. I bet you will never see him again. If that boy comes back, I'll eat my hat!"

Mr. Brownlow was not pleased with his friend's words. "Oliver is not a thief," he said, "so get ready to eat your hat. Oliver *will* be back!"

When Oliver neared the bookstore, he saw Nancy. Nancy was Fagin's good friend. He had often heard Nancy and Fagin whispering. She was with a man Oliver had never seen before. The man was a thief named Bill Sikes.

"Oh, Bill," cried Nancy, "there is my long, lost brother!" she shouted, running toward Oliver. She threw her arms around Oliver and held on tight.

Oliver didn't know what she was up to. But he knew she was up to something. "Help! Help!" Oliver shouted, as Nancy and Bill began to beat him and pull him along.

A man passing by stopped to help Oliver. Nancy told him, "He doesn't need your help. He's my brother, and he's trying to run away. He's nothing but a little thief!"

The man looked at Oliver, then at Nancy and Bill. Believing her story, the man walked away.

Nancy and Bill took Oliver back to Fagin's place. Oliver tried to get away, but Nancy and Bill had a tight hold on him.

Fagin's place was as dirty as ever. How Oliver wished he had not left Mr. Brownlow's clean, quiet house. He cried and cried. He begged and begged. "*Please*," said Oliver, "I must return Mr. Brownlow's money, or he will think I'm a thief!"

Fagin just laughed at Oliver. Then he grabbed a big stick, ready to beat the frightened boy.

"Stop! Don't beat him," Nancy begged. "He's had enough already."

Fagin put down the stick. He told Bill to lock Oliver up. But before he did, Fagin took way Oliver's new clothes. He gave him old rags to wear. "We can get money for these nice clothes," he said, laughing.

Once again, Oliver was all alone. He didn't feel very good. Could it be that he was getting sick again? He closed his eyes. "Dear God," said Oliver, in a whisper, "please, I don't want Mr. Brownlow to think I ran away with his money. Please help me, God."

Oliver laid his head down on the hard floor. He missed his soft pillow back at Mr. Brownlow's place. He missed the soft brush of Mrs. Bedwin's hand. As he thought on these things, Oliver began to cry. *Will I ever find a real home?* he thought.

More Trouble For Oliver

COMPREHENSION CHECK

Choose the best answer.

1. Mrs. Bedwin worked for
   _____a. Fagin.
   _____b. Mr. Brownlow.
   _____c. Mr. Grimwig.
   _____d. the doctor.

2. What was it that had left Oliver feeling very sick?
   _____a. A bad cold
   _____b. Something he ate
   _____c. He was bitten by a bug.
   _____d. The beating he had gotten at the bookstore

3. What did Oliver like best about living at Mr. Brownlow's?
   _____a. Mrs. Bedwin's cooking
   _____b. Mr. Brownlow's books
   _____c. The house was very clean and neat.
   _____d. Mr. Brownlow's paintings

4. Oliver thought the woman in the painting that hung in the library
   _____a. looked like his mother.
   _____b. was Mr. Brownlow's wife.
   _____c. was Mr. Grimwig's daughter.
   _____d. was looking at him.

5. Oliver tried hard to
   _____a. be a good boy.
   _____b. get on Mr. Brownlow's good side.
   _____c. get even with Fagin.
   _____d. make money to get his own place.

6. Nancy and Bill Sikes
   _____a. were Oliver's good friends.
   _____b. were clever theives who were working for Fagin.
   _____c. were poor people just trying to make a living..
   _____d. were Mr. Brownlow's friendly neighbors.

7. Why did Nancy and Bill Sikes take Oliver back to Fagin's?
   _____a. They missed him.
   _____b. They knew that Fagin was looking for him.
   _____c. Oliver wanted to go back with them.
   _____d. Charley Bates and Jack Dawkins missed him.

8. Before Bill Sikes locked Oliver up,
   _____a. Fagin took away Oliver's new clothes.
   _____b. Fagin beat Oliver with a big stick.
   _____c. Fagin took Mr. Brownlow's money away from Oliver.
   _____d. Nancy gave him something to eat.

9. Another name for this story could be
   _____a. "Back at Fagin's."
   _____b. "The Big Lie."
   _____c. "Oliver Grows Up."
   _____d. "Nancy Finds Her Brother."

10. This story is mainly about
    _____a. why Oliver ran away from Mr. Brownlow's.
    _____b. a doctor who saved Oliver's life.
    _____c. how trouble always seemed to follow Oliver.
    _____d. why Mrs. Bedwin liked Oliver so much.

Check your answers with the key on page 67.

More Trouble For Oliver

VOCABULARY CHECK

brush	healthy	laid	pillow	tight	wipe

I. Sentences to Finish

Fill in the blank in each sentence with the correct key word from the box above.

1. Mom sleeps with one _____; Dad sleeps with two.

2. The lost girl held on _____ to the policeman's hand.

3. It is said that eating an apple a day will keep you _____.

4. Tim lost his car keys. He thought he _____ them on the table.

5. "_____ off your shoes before coming into the house," said Mother.

6. With the soft _____ of her hand, Mother wiped away her tears.

II. Matching

Write the letter of the correct meaning from Column B next to the key word in Column A.

Column A		Column B
1. brush	_____	a. to take (away, off, or out) by rubbing
2. healthy	_____	b. put down; lay down
3. laid	_____	c. firmly
4. pillow	_____	d. remove or wipe away
5. tight	_____	e. a bag or case filled with soft material
6. wipe	_____	f. feeling well; not sick

Check your answers with the key on page 70.

This page may be reproduced for classroom use.

THE ROBBERY

PREPARATION

Key Words

against	(ə genst´)	1. upon; pushing (leaning) on something else *Judy leaned the rake <u>against</u> the fence.*
		2. in opposition to; not in favor of *Cindy fought <u>against</u> the new law.*
husband	(huz´ bənd)	a man who has a wife *Sarah and her <u>husband</u> went to dinner.*
lying	(lī´ ing)	1. not telling the truth *Mother can always tell when I'm <u>lying</u>.* 2. The cat is <u>lying</u> on the floor; Sue is <u>lying</u> in her bed; Dad is <u>lying</u> down.
planned	(pland)	worked out an idea or plan beforehand *Ann <u>planned</u> a party for her sister.*
rich	(rich)	1. having much money, land, or goods *Harry's latest book made him a <u>rich</u> man.* 2. costly; expensive *Sam lives in a <u>rich</u> neighborhood.*
we're	(wir)	we are *<u>We're</u> going to a football game today.*

THE ROBBERY

Necessary Words

gun   (gun)   a weapon that shoots bullets
                                            The thief carried a <u>gun</u> under his coat.

information   (in´ fər mā´shən)   knowledge; news; facts
                                            *The book gave me a lot of <u>information</u> on
                                            deep-sea fishing.*

niece   (nēs)   the daugher of one's brother or sister
                                            Julie and her <u>niece</u> are coming to visit.

reward   (ri wôrd´)   something given (usually money) in return
                                            for information or the return of something
                                            Randy got a <u>reward</u> for finding the lost dog.

robbery   (rob´ ər e)   theft; stealing
                                            The <u>robbery</u> took place at ten o'clock.

servant   (ser´vənt)   a person who works in another's home
                                            Miss Lily's <u>servant</u> is a fine cook.

shot   (shot)   hit by bullets from a gun
                                            The deer had been <u>shot</u> in its leg.

THE ROBBERY

Mr. Bumble takes the reward money.

Preview:
1. Read the name of the story.
2. Look at the picture.
3. Read the sentence under the picture.
4. Read the first four paragraphs of the story.
5. Then answer the following question.

You learned from your preview that Mr. Bumble
____a. knew where to find Oliver.
____b. did not know where Oliver was.
____c. didn't want the reward money.
____d. had good things to say about Oliver.

Turn to the Comprehension Check on page 34 for the right answer.

Now read the story.

Read to find out how Oliver gets hurt.

THE ROBBERY

Mr. Brownlow was sad that Oliver did not come back from the bookstore. But he still would not believe Oliver a thief! He went to the office of the town paper. He ran these words: **WANTED: ANY INFORMATION THAT WILL HELP ME FIND OLIVER TWIST. $REWARD$**

When Mr. Bumble read the paper, a smile crossed his face. He marched over to Mr. Brownlow's house. "Oliver is a very bad boy," he told Mr. Brownlow. "He has done terrible things. But I think I know where you can find him," he lied. He gave him the name of a place outside of town. He knew Mr. Brownlow would not find Oliver there. But he really didn't care...as long as he got the reward money.

"I had planned to give you a lot more money," said Mr. Brownlow. "But you have not had kind things to say about the boy. But thank you for letting me know where I can find him." He handed the reward to Mr. Bumble.

Mr. Bumble took the money. He was not sorry for lying about where to find Oliver. But he was sorry for lying about Oliver being a bad boy. *If only I had said something good about the boy,* he thought. *I would be holding more money right now!*

Back at Fagin's, Oliver was learning to become a thief. Over and over, Fagin made him play the game of picking pockets. But Oliver didn't like the game. "You will do what I tell you to do," Fagin told him. "Or you will get it!"

One night, Bill Sikes told Fagin, "I have planned a robbery in a rich part of town. I have looked the house over. At night, everything is closed up tight. But there is a small window that a young boy like Oliver can get through."

The next day Nancy came to get Oliver. "We're going to Bill Sike's place," she told him. "Do as he tells you and you won't get hurt." She showed Oliver her arms and neck. There were black and blue marks on them. "Bill will hurt us both if you don't listen," she said.

Oliver did not think much of Nancy. But she did keep Fagin from beating him, once. And she had tried hard to keep Oliver out of this robbery. But her black and blue marks still hurt. She knew better than to go against Bill's wishes.

Bill and Oliver met up with two other men. "We're going to rob some rich people," he said.

"*Please* don't make me rob anyone," Oliver begged.

Bill held a gun against Oliver's head. "If you whisper a word inside the house," he said, "you will be shot!"

After dark, Oliver and the other men went to the rich house. Inside, everyone was sleeping. Bill made Oliver crawl through the small window. "Rob all you can," he told Oliver. "And remember, I will use this gun on you if you say one word."

All along, Oliver had planned to get caught. He didn't want to rob anyone. But now he was having second thoughts. He believed Bill would use his gun. And he didn't want to die.

Quietly, Oliver moved around the house. But he tripped on something in the dark. The noise woke someone up. "Who's there?" a man shouted, as he lighted a candle.

Outside, Bill saw the light. He heard someone at the window. He pointed his gun in the dark, but before he fired, he heard a loud *BANG!* Oliver fell back. He had been shot! He felt the blood rushing from his arm. But he got up and started to climb out the window. Bill caught hold of Oliver's foot and pulled him outside. Bill ran fast, pulling Oliver behind. But Oliver could not keep up. When Bill felt they were far enough away, he let go of Oliver's hand. Bill kept on running. He didn't look back to see Oliver fall to the ground.

Oliver woke up several hours later. He wondered how long he had been lying in the dirt. His arm hurt badly. Blood was still running from where he had been hit. Oliver got up and ran to the nearest house. He didn't know it, but it was the same house that he had tried to rob.

"Help!" cried Oliver, as he banged on the door. One of the servants opened the door. When she saw Oliver's arm, she called for her husband.

"This must be the robber I shot," he said. He called for the lady of the house, Mrs. Maylie. Mrs. Maylie and her niece Rose, came running. They took one look at Oliver and called the doctor.

As the doctor worked on Oliver's arm, Oliver looked around the room. *What a rich home,* he thought. He looked over at Mrs. Maylie. She was talking to a beautiful, young girl. Oliver couldn't take his eyes off her. *I wonder if she has a husband,* he thought.

Though Oliver didn't know it, Rose and her aunt were talking about him. "He doesn't look like a thief to me," said Rose. Mrs. Maylie didn't think so, either. "Maybe he was not the one who *planned* the robbery," she said, softly.

Against the wishes of Mrs. Maylie's servants, Oliver was made to feel at home. The servants thought Oliver should be sent to jail. But Rose and her aunt wanted to help the boy.

"We must think of something before the police come," said Mrs. Maylie, to her niece. "Maybe we can talk the servants out of telling their story. Let's get them to think that they made a mistake. We'll get them to think that Oliver was *not* one of the robbers."

THE ROBBERY

COMPREHENSION CHECK

Choose the best answer.

Preview Answer:
b. did not know where Oliver was.

(1.) Mr. Brownlow
____a. wanted Oliver to go to jail.
____b. didn't care if he never saw Oliver again.
____c. wanted to give Oliver a reward.
____d. was worried about Oliver.

2. Why did Bill Sikes want Oliver to help in the robbery?
____a. He got along with Oliver.
____b. He needed the help of another person.
____c. Oliver was small enough to climb in the window.
____d. Oliver knew how to use a gun.

(3.) Nancy
____a. got along with Bill Sikes.
____b. was afraid of Bill Sikes.
____c. wanted to Marry Bill Sikes.
____d. was Bill Sike's sister.

(4.) Nancy tried to
____a. talk Bill Sikes out of taking Oliver along.
____b. bring Oliver back to Mr. Brownlow's.
____c. tell the police about the robbery.
____d. hide Bill Sike's gun.

(5.) First, Oliver and the other men went to the rich house. Then Oliver climbed through the window. Next,
____a. a shot rang out.
____b. Oliver tripped on something in the dark.
____c. Someone lighted a candle.
____d. Bill Sikes ran.

(6.) Who shot Oliver?
____a. Bill Sikes
____b. Fagin
____c. One of Mrs. Maylie's servants
____d. A policeman

7. How long had Oliver been lying in the dirt before he ran for help?
____a. Several hours
____b. Several days
____c. Several minutes
____d. Five minutes

8 Mrs. Maylie and her niece Rose
____a. had never seen a real thief before.
____b. called the police to come and take Oliver away.
____c. did not think Oliver had planned the robbery.
____d. thought Oliver was a clever boy.

9. Another name for this story could be
____a. "A Shot in the Dark."
____b. "A Lovely Rose."
____c. "The Reward."
____d. "Going Home."

10. This story is mainly about
____a. a robbery that went wrong.
____b. how Oliver ended up in more trouble.
____c. how Nancy tried to keep Oliver out of trouble.
____d. robbing rich people.

Check your answers with the key on page 67.

This page may be reproduced for classroom use.

THE ROBBERY

VOCABULARY CHECK

against	husband	lying	planned	rich	we're

I. Sentences to Finish
Fill in the blank in each sentence with the correct key word from the box above.

1. Johnny wants to know if _____ going to the game on Saturday.

2. "Don't lean _____ the fence, I just painted it!" said Dad.

3. The _____ woman lived in a grand, old house.

4. We _____ a party for Mother's birthday.

5. "Stop _____!" shouted Dave, "and tell me the truth!"

6. Jenny and her _____ bought a new house.

II. Using the Words

On the lines below, write six of your own sentences using the key words from the box above. Use each word once, drawing a line under the key word.

1. _____

2. _____

3. _____

4. _____

5. _____

6. _____

Check your answers with the key on page 70.

This page may be reproduced for classroom use.

A CHANGE FOR OLIVER

PREPARATION

Key Words

beyond	(bi yond´)	farther away; farther on than *I saw a lake just <u>beyond</u> the house.*
company	(kum´ pə nē)	a group of people joined together for some purpose *Harry kept <u>company</u> with some bad people.*
depend	(di pend´)	rely; trust *Can I <u>depend</u> on you to help me out?*
disappoint	(dis´ ə point´)	fail to satisfy one's wish or hope *"Please don't <u>disappoint</u> me by coming in late," said Mother.*
doesn't	(duz´ nt)	does not *Jack <u>doesn't</u> know how to swim.*
shadow	(shad´ ō)	a shade made by some person or thing *When I turned on the light, I saw my <u>shadow</u> on the wall.*

A CHANGE FOR OLIVER

Necessary Words

alive (ə līv´) living; having life
The man who was shot is very much <u>alive</u>.

church (chėrch) a building where one goes to hear about God
Our family goes to <u>church</u> every week.

learned (lėrnd) found out about new things
*The children <u>learned</u> many new things
in school today.*

rent (rent) money paid to live in or use another's property
Sam pays the <u>rent</u> on time every month.

son (sun) a boy child
The man took his <u>son</u> fishing.

People

Monks is a man who keeps company with Fagin. He holds a dark secret
about Oliver.

A CHANGE FOR OLIVER

Nancy tells Fagin, "Oliver will be better off dead than being around company like you!"

Preview:
    1. Read the name of the story.
    2. Look at the picture.
    3. Read the sentence under the picture.
    4. Read the first five paragraphs of the story.
    5. Then answer the following question.

After learning that Oliver had been shot, Fagin
____a. went out for a drink.
____b. went looking for Monks.
____c. went looking for Oliver.
____d. beat up Bill Sikes.

Turn to the Comprehension Check on page 40 for the right answer.

Now read the story.

Read to find out why Fagin and Monks want Oliver to get into trouble.

A CHANGE FOR OLIVER

Late that night, two men were telling Fagin about the robbery. "It didn't work out," said one of the men. "Oliver is lying on the ground, just beyond the house. Don't be too surprised, Fagin, if you find him dead."

"You disappoint me!" shouted Fagin. "I thought I could depend on both of you!" The two men looked down at the floor. They didn't mean to disappoint Fagin. They just wanted to let him know what had happened. Fagin left the room, slamming the door behind him.

Fagin hurried to an eating and drinking place where he kept company with other bad men. He looked for Monks, but Monks was not there.

"When he comes," Fagin told a friend, "tell him I must see him right away. I'll depend on you to keep this a secret." Fagin left to find Bill Sikes and Nancy.

Nancy was not happy to see Fagin. The more she saw him, the less she liked him. "Oliver will be better off dead than being around company like you," she told Fagin.

Fagin smiled. "There's more money for me if Oliver stays alive," he said coldly.

Fagin started home, and on the way he ran into Monks. "Come with me," Fagin said. "We must talk in secret."

At Fagin's place, Monks followed Fagin down a long, dark hall. When they reached the stairs, they thought they heard something. The noise frightened both of them. They were supposed to be alone. Fagin and Monks looked around, but all the boys were sleeping. Finding no

one, Fagin and Monks went up the stairs to a little room. Fagin shut the door. He told Monks that Oliver had been shot.

"I want Oliver alive," whispered Monks. "I want him to rob and get caught. Then I will get what is mine. But if he dies, that's okay, too. I'm getting sick and tired of Oliver Twist!"

Fagin didn't like what he was hearing. "But if Oliver dies," said Fagin, "all our work has been for nothing. It will be much better for us if he stays alive. Then we'll both be rich! I think we should stick with our first plan. Teach the boy how to rob, and let him get caught. Yes, I think that's best. What do you say, Monks?"

"Sure, sure," said Monks. "But you have tried to teach him to rob. And has he learned anything? I think not. Seems to me that Oliver can do no wrong. He always finds his way out of troub..."

Suddenly, Monks stopped talking. He thought he saw a woman's shadow on the wall. Monks and Fagin looked around, but again, they found no one.

"We better get some rest," said Fagin. "First we thought we heard someone. Now we're seeing shadows. Let's call it a night, Monks. We'll talk again some other time."

* * * *

Back at Mrs. Maylie's, Oliver was getting better. Mrs. Maylie had told the police that Oliver had been shot by a robber. The police had no reason not to believe her story, so they left.

She had called the doctor, who had come right over. He had taken

good care of Oliver's leg.

"You can stay with us as long as you like, Oliver," said Mrs. Maylie. "If you like, you can come with us to the country. We have a beautiful place there."

"You are so kind to me," Oliver said. "When I'm well again, I'll help you all I can. I only wish I could see Mr. Brownlow again. Then I could tell him what happened to his money – the money I was taking to the bookstore. I don't want him to think I'm a thief."

The next day Mrs. Maylie took Oliver to Mr. Brownlow's place. But when they got there, they saw a sign on the grass. The sign said, "FOR RENT". Mr. Brownlow had left the country for awhile. He had put up his house for rent while he was away.

Summer came and Mrs. Maylie, Rose, and Oliver left for the country. There, Oliver ran in the fields. He learned the names of birds and flowers. Each day he went to see a kind, old man who taught him to read. Oliver learned many new things. In return for Mrs. Maylie's kindness, Oliver worked hard to help Mrs. Maylie. In just a few weeks, Oliver was strong and healthy again.

Mrs. Maylie took Oliver to church. In church, Oliver learned about God. There, he met many boys who were poor. But they were not like the poor boys who kept company with Fagin. These boys were clean, kind, and worked very hard.

Oliver had never been so happy. But his troubles with Fagin and his company were far from over.

A CHANGE FOR OLIVER

COMPREHENSION CHECK

Choose the best answer.

1. Who told Fagin that Oliver had been shot?
   ____a. Nancy
   ____b. Bill Sikes
   ____c. Monks
   ____d. Two men

2. Fagin was angry with the two men because
   ____a. they always disappointed him.
   ____b. the robbery didn't go as planned.
   ____c. they had left Oliver for dead.
   ____d. they had come over late at night.

3. Fagin and Monks
   ____a. liked each other.
   ____b. lived together.
   ____c. shared a secret about Oliver.
   ____d. wanted the best for Oliver.

4. Monks only cared about
   ____a. Fagin.
   ____b. Oliver.
   ____c. being kind to everyone.
   ____d. money.

5. Where did Fagin and Monks go to talk about their secret?
   ____a. To the park
   ____b. To Monks's drinking place
   ____c. To Fagin's place
   ____d. To Monks's house

Preview Answer:

b. went looking for Monks.

6. First Fagin and Monks heard a noise. Then Monks thought he saw someone's shadow. Next,
   ____a. they heard someone creeping up the stairs.
   ____b. Monks headed for the door.
   ____c. Fagin and Monks called the police.
   ____d. Fagin decided to talk again some other time.

7. Mrs. Maylie told the police that Oliver
   ____a. had been shot by a robber.
   ____b. had shot himself.
   ____c. was her son.
   ____d. was her brother.

8. In the country,
   ____a. Oliver met many boys just like himself.
   ____b. Oliver taught an old man how to read.
   ____c. Oliver got sick again.
   ____d. Mrs. Maylie made Oliver work very hard.

9. Another name for this story could be
   ____a. "Mr. Brownlow Leaves the Country."
   ____b. "A Day in the Country."
   ____c. "A Dark Secret."
   ____d. "Shadows on the Wall."

10. This story is mainly about
   ____a. Fagin and Monks's plan for Oliver.
   ____b. why Nancy did not like Fagin.
   ____c. how Oliver learned to read.
   ____d. Oliver making new friends.

Check your answers with the key on page 67.

This page may be reproduced for classroom use.

A CHANGE FOR OLIVER

VOCABULARY CHECK

beyond	company	depend	disappoint	doesn't	shadow

I. Sentences to Finish
Fill in the blank in each sentence with the correct key word from the box above.

1. "If you don't come to my party, you will _____ me," said Sally.

2. Mother won't let me keep _____ with boys who wear long hair.

3. Larry _____ know how to drive a car.

4. The boy's _____ seemed to follow him as he walked.

5. Ron lives just _____ the bridge.

6. I told Dad he could _____ on me to help him with the yard.

II. Word Search
All the words from the box above are hidden in the puzzle below. They may be written from left to right, right to left, or on an angle. As you find each word, put a circle around it. One word, that is not a key word, has been done for you.

```
D  I  S  A  P  P  O  I  N  T
C  X  H  B  E  Y  C  S  D  E
O  W  A  I  D  A  H  S  B  B
M  E  D  O  E  S  N  T  E  B
P  C  O  M  P  A  N  Y  Y  A
D  O  W  C  E  T  O  X  O  D
I  U  C  O  N  N  O  C  S  I
S  H  A  D  D  A  P  P  H  S
```

Check your answers with the key on page 70.

This page may be reproduced for classroom use.

The Locket

PREPARATION

Key Words

became	(bi kām´)	came to be *Joe became angry when he lost the game.*
become	(bi kum´)	come to be *Isaac is going to become a doctor.*
below	(bi lō´)	down low, or in a lower place *Your foot is below your knee.*
famous	(fā´ məs)	very well known *A famous football player will be visiting our school next week.*
flow	(flō)	to move along steadily in a stream *The flow of city traffic can make me late for work.*
mind	(mīnd)	the part of a person that thinks, knows, learns, remembers, and understands *"Please keep your mind on the job you're doing," said Mother.*

The Locket

Necessary Words

buggy   (bug´ ē)   a light carriage with one seat
Mr. Smith came to town in a horse and <u>buggy</u>.

inn   (in)   a place where people eat and sleep when away from home
The <u>inn</u> was famous for its clean rooms and good food.

locket   (lok´ it)   a little case worn on a chain around the neck
Jane wore a <u>locket</u> around her neck.

meanwhile   (mēn hwīl´)   in or during the time between
Dad painted the house; <u>meanwhile</u>, I cut the grass.

The Locket

Oliver pays for a horse and rider to take him to a doctor in London.

Preview: 1. Read the name of the story.
2. Look at the picture.
3. Read the sentence under the picture.
4. Read the first four paragraphs of the story.
5. Then answer the following question.

You learned from your preview that
____a. Mrs. Maylie needed a doctor.
____b. many people were looking for Oliver.
____c. Oliver could run very fast.
____d. Oliver loved horses.

Turn to the Comprehension Check on page 46 for the right answer.

Now read the story.

Read to find out about the secret inside the locket.

The Locket

One night, Rose became very sick. Her head was very warm and she felt very weak. Mrs. Maylie put Rose to bed and watched her carefully through the night. In the morning, Rose was not any better. Her head was much warmer and her color was very white.

Mrs. Maylie called Oliver. "Oliver," she said, "hurry to the village. Send this letter to my son Harry, then get to the doctor in London. Here is some money for the ride, and here is the doctor's address. And please hurry. Rose needs a doctor, *fast!*"

Oliver ran all the way to the village inn. There, he sent the letter and paid someone to take him to London.

As Oliver stood outside the inn waiting for his ride, a mean-looking man came out of the inn. "*You!*" he shouted. "You must be little Oliver!" Mean words began to flow from the man's mouth. Oliver became frightened. He was just about to run home, when the horse and buggy arrived. Oliver jumped in the seat and headed for London.

Two days later, Oliver and the doctor arrived. The doctor took good care of Rose. Her fever began to disappear. The color returned to her face. When Mrs. Maylie's son, Harry, arrived, Rose's face seemed to light up like the sun.

"I was so worried for you, Rose," said Harry. "I got here as soon as I could."

"There was no need for you to hurry," said Rose, smiling. "As you can see, my health has returned."

"But I love you, Rose," said Harry, reaching for her hand. "I don't know what I would do without you."

Soon the days turned happy. Rose returned to good health. Mrs. Maylie went back to working in her garden. And Oliver and Harry became good friends.

One day Oliver sat reading by his window, when he fell fast asleep. In his mind, he saw Fagin and the angry man from the inn. Then, half-awake, he saw them both at his window. Oliver shouted for Harry. Everyone in the house came running. When Oliver told them what he had seen, they looked everywhere for the men. But they found no sign of anyone.

The day came when it was time for Harry to return to work. But first, he would ask Rose to become his wife.

"I love you," he said to Rose. "I love you and want you to become my wife."

Rose put her head down. She did not want to look at Harry. "I would love to have you for a husband," she said. "But I know you will become famous, one day. Then you will want a wife who is from a famous family. But me? I don't even know who my mother and father were," she said, sadly.

But Harry wouldn't give up. "I don't care who your mother and father were, or where you came from. And being famous is not important to me. All I know is that you are a good woman, and I love you."

But Rose's mind was made up. Smiling, she said good-bye to Harry, but her heart was very sad. As Harry got into the buggy, he looked back at Rose. "I'll be back again in a year," he said. "And I hope by then, you will have changed your mind."

As the buggy pulled away, Rose wiped her wet eyes. She went back into the house, looking for Oliver. Oliver always had a way of making her feel good.

* * * *

Meanwhile, Mr. Bumble and his new wife (who once worked at the workhouse), were in London. They were on their way to meet someone at an old building. Below the building, ran a fast-flowing river. Inside the building, they met Monks.

"I have something to show you, Monks," said Mrs. Bumble. "I heard that you were looking for this. But before I show you, I want a little money first."

Monks made a face. He didn't like this woman at all. But if she had what he was looking for, that didn't matter. He reached into his pocket and pulled out some money. He handed the money to Mrs. Bumble. "Go on," he said. "Let's see what you've got."

Mrs. Bumble reached into her bag. She pulled out a shiny, gold locket and handed it over to Monks. "The night Oliver was born," she said, "a woman took a gold locket from his dying mother. This is that locket. I got it at a shop that sells new and used things."

Monks opened the locket. Inside, was a sparkling, gold ring. Printed on the inside of the ring was the name *AGNES*. This was the name of Oliver's mother. Monks broke into a smile. His mouth seemed to stretch from ear to ear.

"Has anyone else seen this?" Monks asked Mrs. Bumble.

"No, sir, I have shown no one."

Monks opened a door in the floor. Below, flowed the fast-flowing river. He threw the locket and ring into the water. "Now, no one but us will ever know about this."

* * * *

Meanwhile, Bill Sikes had become very sick. Nancy took good care of him, but he was as mean as ever. He hit Nancy if she didn't do things just the way he wanted. He hit her if she didn't move as fast as he wanted her to. As Nancy fixed Bill something to eat, she heard a knock at the door. It was Fagin.

"I'm glad to see you, Fagin," said Bill. "I'm almost out of money. I need some more today."

"I just stopped by to see how you were doing," said Fagin. "I have no money with me. Nancy can come home with me and get it. Let me know when you're better so you can get back to work." Nancy was glad to be leaving with Fagin. Anything was better than staying with Bill.

While Nancy was at Fagin's, Monks stopped by. He and Fagin went to another room and closed the door. Nancy took off her shoes and quietly walked over to the door. She put her ear to the door and listened. What she heard made her hurry back to Bill's.

Nancy fixed Bill something to drink. She put something in the drink that would make Bill very sleepy. When she knew that Bill was sound asleep, she rented a horse and buggy.

"*Quick!*" she said to the driver. She showed him a piece of paper with an address on it. "Take me to his house," she said. "And make it *fast!*"

45

The Locket

COMPREHENSION CHECK

Choose the best answer.

1. Why did Mrs. Maylie send Oliver for the doctor?
   ____a. She did not feel well.
   ____b. Her son was not well.
   ____c. Rose was very sick.
   ____d. She wanted the doctor to come over for dinner.

2. What do you think was in the letter that Mrs. Maylie had Oliver mail to her son?
   ____a. Money
   ____b. News that Rose was very sick
   ____c. News that Oliver was being a good boy
   ____d. Her will

3. Oliver and the doctor arrived at Mrs. Maylie's
   ____a. the next day.
   ____b. in five days.
   ____c. in one week.
   ____d. in two days.

4. Harry
   ____a. was in love with Rose.
   ____b. did not like Mrs. Maylie.
   ____c. did not like Oliver.
   ____d. did not care much for the doctor.

5. Rose would not marry Harry because
   ____a. she knew she wouldn't make a good wife.
   ____b. she thought Harry would make a poor husband.
   ____c. she didn't think she was good enough for Harry.
   ____d. he didn't give her a ring.

6. Who had the locket that Monks had been looking for?
   ____a. Mrs. Bumble
   ____b. Oliver
   ____c. Nancy
   ____d. Mrs. Maylie

7. What secret did the locket hold?
   ____a. Where Monks's family was
   ____b. The name of Oliver's mother
   ____c. The name of Oliver's father
   ____d. Why Oliver's mother had died

8. Who was Oliver's mother?
   ____a. Agatha
   ____b. Anna
   ____c. Anita
   ____d. Agnes

9. Another name for this story could be
   ____a. "Oliver Finds His Mother."
   ____b. "A Dark Secret."
   ____c. "Harry Falls In Love."
   ____d. "Harry Becomes Famous."

10. This story is mainly about
    ____a. the secret of who Oliver's mother was.
    ____b. how Rose almost died.
    ____c. why Rose and Harry would never get married.
    ____d. Oliver's days in the country.

Check your answers with the key on page 67.

This page may be reproduced for classroom use.

The Locket

VOCABULARY CHECK

became	become	below	famous	flow	mind

I. Sentences to Finish
Fill in the blank in each sentence with the correct key word from the box above.

1. We watched the empty boat _____ down the river.

2. Peter _____ the leader of the band.

3. We couldn't talk Laura into going to the party. Her _____ was made up.

4. What will _____ of my little lost dog?

5. Amos's cookies made him a _____ man.

6. From my window, I watched the children playing in the street _____ .

II. Using the Words
On the lines below, write six of your own sentences using the key words from the box above. Use each word once, drawing a line under the key word.

1. _____

2. _____

3. _____

4. _____

5. _____

6. _____

Check your answers with the key on page 71.

More Secrets

PREPARATION

Key Words

eleven   (i lev´ ən)   the number after ten and before twelve
We need <u>eleven</u> players for the game.

helping   (hel´ ping)   aiding; assisting; giving help to
Sandy was <u>helping</u> the old woman in her garden.

hug   (hug)   put the arms around and hold close
Maria gave a big <u>hug</u> to her grandmother.

meet   (mēt)   get together with; come face to face with
Joe will <u>meet</u> his friends at the river.

steal   (stēl)   to take something that does not belong to you
"That man tried to <u>steal</u> the lady's purse."

though   (thō)   even if
<u>Though</u> it's raining, we're still going to the beach.

More Secrets

Necessary Words

danger	(dān´ jər)	the chance that something bad or harmful may happen
		We knew the <u>danger</u> in skating on the lake's thin ice.

midnight	(mid´ nīt´)	twelve o'clock at night
		At <u>midnight</u>, we heard a loud knock at the door.

Sunday	(sun´ dē)	the first day of the week
		Our family goes to church every <u>Sunday</u>.

warn	(wôrn)	give notice to; put on guard against danger
		It was my job to <u>warn</u> the children to fasten their seat belts.

Things

London Bridge   is a famous bridge in the city of London.

More Secrets

Nancy warns Rose that Oliver is in danger.

Preview:
1. Read the name of the story.
2. Look at the picture.
3. Read the sentence under the picture.
4. Read the first six paragraphs of the story.
5. Then answer the following question.

You learned from your preview that
____a. Rose and Monks were very good friends.
____b. Rose had never heard of Monks.
____c. Nancy was in danger.
____d. Mrs. Maylie's servant did not like Nancy.

Turn to the Comprehension Check on page 52 for the right answer.

Now read the story.

Read to find out who Monks turns out to be.

More Secrets

Mrs. Maylie, Rose and Oliver left the country and went back to London. It was at Mrs. Maylie's house that Nancy came at midnight.

"I must warn Rose," Nancy said to the servant who answered the door. "I must warn her that Oliver is in danger."

The servant hurried Nancy inside to meet Rose. Nancy talked very fast. "Oliver is in danger," she told Rose. "Fagin and Monks know that he is here."

"*Monks?*" asked Rose, with a puzzled look.

"You mean you never heard of him?" asked Nancy.

"Why, no," answered Rose. "Should I know him?"

Nancy kept on talking. "Well, he knows who you are. And he knows a lot about little Oliver. It's all very strange," said Nancy, "but Monks is out to get him. I don't know why, but Monks wants Oliver to learn to steal. He wants him to go to jail."

Rose could not believe her ears. "But why would this Monks want Oliver to go to jail?" she asked Nancy.

"I really don't know all the answers," said Nancy. "I tried to find out one night when Monks and Fagin were talking. But when they saw my shadow on the wall, I ran. I got away just in time. Then tonight, they met again. I listened at the door. I heard Monks say that no one will ever know who Oliver's mother is. The locket that tells is lying at the bottom of the river. And..." Nancy's voice became a whisper, "...Monks is Oliver's half-brother!"

Rose's eyes grew very big. "*What did you say?*"

"Yes, Rose, yes! Oliver and Monks have the same father. Like I said, I don't have all the answers, just yet. But little Oliver is in danger. Monks is doing everything he can to get Oliver to steal...to go to jail. So please watch out for Oliver. I'm afraid that Monks will come here and try to take him back to Fagin's place."

Rose looked a little frightened. "Thank you for coming to warn us, Nancy."

"You'll hear from me again," said Nancy. "I'm not through helping yet. But I must hurry home now, or I'll be in danger, too."

Rose got up from her chair. "Don't go, Nancy. You can stay with us. We'll help you begin a new life. I'm sure Mrs. Maylie wouldn't mind."

"No, kind lady. It is too late for me. My home is with Bill Sikes. Even though it's not the best life, it's the one I'm used to. And though Bill Sikes is mean to me, I can't say that I don't love him."

"Can I give you any money for your trouble?" asked Rose.

Nancy laughed. "Though I could use the money, I must say no. I came here to warn you about Monks and Fagin. Nothing more...nothing less. But thank you, Rose. I must be going now."

"But when will I see you again?" asked Rose.

"If I'm still alive, I will be walking on London Bridge between eleven and midnight each Sunday. You can meet me then. But don't come alone. You never know what danger might be hiding in the darkness. I'll let you know if I hear any more about Oliver and his mother."

Nancy ran out of the house and got into the buggy. Bill was still sleeping when she got home.

The next morning, Oliver hurried in to see Rose. "Someone saw Mr. Brownlow! He's back from his trip!"

"Then we'll go see him right now," said Rose. She and a servant took Oliver in a horse and buggy to Mr. Brownlow's house. Rose asked Oliver to wait in the buggy while she went in to talk to Mr. Brownlow first. She wanted Mr. Brownlow's help.

Mr. Brownlow and Mr. Grimwig were in the sitting room. Rose quickly told them that Oliver did not steal Mr. Brownlow's money...that he was on his way to the bookstore when he was caught and brought back to

Fagin's. Then she told them about her meeting with Nancy. She warned them of the danger little Oliver was in.

Mr. Brownlow told Rose not to worry. "Mr. Grimwig will be helping us," he said. "He is a very wise man."

Just then, Mrs. Bedwin and Oliver came into the room. Oliver ran to Mr. Brownlow. He gave him a big hug. Mr. Brownlow hugged him back. "It's so good to see you again, Oliver," he said.

* * * *

Meanwhile, Noah Claypole had come to London. He wasn't there long, before Fagin put him back to work. "I think Nancy is up to something," he said. "I want you to follow her every move."

On the next Sunday evening, Fagin stopped over to see Bill Sikes. "I haven't seen you for a while," said Fagin. "Are you still sick?"

"Oh, I'm still sick," said Bill. "If Nancy, here, would take better care of me, I would be up and about."

Nancy made a face at Bill. But Fagin shot Nancy an even meaner look. Nancy began to worry. It was after eleven. She had to get to the bridge before midnight.

"Bill, I'm going outside for some fresh air," she said, reaching for her coat.

"Sit down, woman!" shouted Bill. "You're not going anywhere. You're staying right here!"

Nancy became frightened at the sound of Bill's voice. She put her coat back in the closet and went into the kitchen. She waited for Fagin to leave, but he was in no hurry. Soon, the clock passed midnight.

Fagin got up to leave. "Keep an eye on Nancy," he told Bill. "That girl is up to no good. If she gets out of hand, *you* will have to answer to me!"

On his way home, Fagin was already making plans for Bill. He never really liked Bill. But he needed Nancy. *If I can find some way to kill Bill,* he thought, *then I will take charge of Nancy.*

More Secrets

COMPREHENSION CHECK

Choose the best answer.

1. Why do you think Nancy always seemed to go out around midnight?
   ____a. That's when Bill Sikes was usually sleeping.
   ____b. She didn't want to get a sunburn.
   ____c. She didn't want Fagin to find her.
   ____d. She didn't want to be followed.

2. Monks wanted Oliver
   ____a. to meet his mother.
   ____b. to have a happy home.
   ____c. to go to church.
   ____d. to go to jail.

3. Nancy went out of her way to
   ____a. frighten Rose.
   ____b. learn the truth about Oliver.
   ____c. get out for some fresh air.
   ____d. become a lady.

4. Rose's eyes grew big when Nancy told her that
   ____a. she was in danger.
   ____b. Oliver was in great danger.
   ____c. Monks was Oliver's father.
   ____d. Monks was Oliver's half-brother.

5. Rose wanted Nancy to
   ____a. leave London.
   ____b. leave the house and never come back.
   ____c. leave Bill Sikes.
   ____d. learn more about Oliver's mother.

6. Nancy told Rose that she could meet her on London Bridge every Sunday
   ____a. between eleven and midnight.
   ____b. at noon.
   ____c. at five o'clock.
   ____d. at eight o'clock.

7. Nancy worried that
   ____a. her own life could be in danger.
   ____b. Oliver would never learn the truth about his mother.
   ____c. Bill would be awake when she got home.
   ____d. Rose didn't believe her story.

8. Fagin
   ____a. did not believe that Bill was sick.
   ____b. wanted nothing to do with Bill or Nancy.
   ____c. wanted Nancy for himself.
   ____d. did not trust Bill to keep Nancy in line.

9. Another name for this story could be
   ____a. "The Midnight Meeting."
   ____b. "Oliver Goes to Jail."
   ____c. "Mr. Brownlow Comes Home."
   ____d. "Noah Claypole Visits London."

10. This story is mainly about
    ____a. why Fagin did not trust Nancy.
    ____b. how Nancy put herself in danger to help Oliver.
    ____c. how Monks took care of his half-brother.
    ____d. Fagin's visit with Bill and Nancy.

Check your answers with the key on page 67.

This page may be reproduced for classroom use.

More Secrets

VOCABULARY CHECK

eleven	helping	hug	meet	steal	though

I. Sentences to Finish
Fill in the blank in each sentence with the correct key word from the box above.

1. Walter thought it was too cold to go swimming, _____ the water was warm.

2. When Jake found his lost dog, he gave him a great big _____ .

3. "Would you mind _____ me wash these dishes?" asked Mother.

4. Tom will _____ his friends at the library.

5. Pam is ten years old. She turns _____ on Tuesday.

6. Sam saw another boy _____ my new bike.

II. Matching
Write the letter of the correct meaning from Column B next to the key word in Column A.

Column A	Column B
_____1. steal	a. take something that doesn't belong to you
_____2. eleven	b. even if
_____3. hug	c. the number after ten and before twelve
_____4. meet	d. aiding; assisting; giving help to
_____5. helping	e. put the arms around and hold close
_____6. though	f. get together with; come face to face with

Check your answers with the key on page 71.

NANCY'S MURDER

PREPARATION

Key Words

drag	(drag)	to pull along slowly *I will <u>drag</u> this big branch to the fire.*
hid	(hid)	to have put something out of sight *The boy <u>hid</u> his bike behind a bush.*
often	(ôf˘ ən)	many times *I <u>often</u> think about leaving the farm.*
spare	(spãr)	1. to stop from hurting someone or taking a life *"<u>Spare</u> my life, Judge, and I'll never steal again."* 2. give *"Please, Sir, can you <u>spare</u> a dime?"*
spot	(spot)	something, such as dirt or color on your clothes, yourself, or on other places *My dog has a big, black <u>spot</u> on its nose.*
struck	(struk)	hit 1. *The clock <u>struck</u> midnight.* 2. *During the fight, the two men <u>struck</u> each other again and again.*

Nancy's Murder

Necessary Words

hate   (hāte)   a very strong feeling of not liking someone or something
1. *I <u>hate</u> cooked vegetables.*
2. *I <u>hate</u> the company he keeps.*

murder   (mėr´ dər)   the planned killing of another person
This week, I read about a <u>murder</u> in our little town.

Nancy's Murder

Nancy wonders if she has been followed.

Preview:
1. Read the name of the story.
2. Look at the picture.
3. Read the sentence under the picture.
4. Read the first three paragraphs of the story.
5. Then answer the following question.

You learned from your preview that Noah Claypole
____a. followed Nancy.
____b. followed Rose.
____c. was afraid of the dark.
____d. liked walking at night.

Turn to the Comprehension Check on page 58 for the right answer.

Now read the story.

Read to find out who takes Nancy's life.

Nancy's Murder

The following Sunday near midnight, Nancy walked on London Bridge. But every few steps, she stopped to look behind her. *Has anyone been following me?* she thought to herself. If someone was following her, it would have been hard to see him. It was very dark at the midnight hour.

Though Nancy had not seen him, Noah Claypole was not far behind. When Nancy took a step, Noah took a step. And each time Nancy stopped, Noah hid himself out of sight.

A few minutes past midnight, a man and a woman appeared on the bridge. When Noah saw them, he quickly went down some steps toward the river. He wasn't sure if he could hide himself from the three of them.

"This is a frightening place to be at such an hour," said the man. "Rose, are you sure we can believe this girl, Nancy?"

"I'm very sure, Mr. Brownlow. Why, there she is right now," she said, pointing to Nancy. They walked over to where Nancy stood waiting.

"I'm very pleased to finally meet you, Nancy," said Mr. Brownlow.

"Sshh," said Nancy, putting her finger to her lips. "We must go below the bridge. I have this feeling that I was followed tonight. I must be sure that no one can hear us."

Mr. Brownlow and Rose followed Nancy down some steps that led to the river. They had no idea that Noah Claypole hid at the river.

They walked at the river's edge for a few minutes. "This is as far as I want to go," said Mr. Brownlow. "Let's talk right here. Nancy, why don't you begin by telling us what this Monks looks like."

"Well, he is very tall and he has this big, red spot on his neck," she began. "He isn't very much to look at, really. But there's one thing about him that will give him away, every time. You see, he often falls on the ground in a fit. And when this happens, his mind kind of goes empty." Then she named the inn

where Monks often went to eat.

Rose was startled. "Why, that sounds like the same man Oliver told me about...the day Oliver ran to the inn to get someone to take him to the doctor for me. That man shouted some very mean words to Oliver. And Oliver said the man had a big, red spot on his neck."

Nancy's eyes began to water. She felt so bad for little Oliver.

"Nancy," said Mr. Brownlow, "let us help you start your life over. We can send you to a far-away country. This man, and his friends, are a danger to you."

"Though I hate my life, I can't do that," said Nancy, sadly. "And like I told Rose, though Bill might not be much of a man, I really do love him. Maybe one day he will love me, too."

When the three had gone, Noah came out from his hiding place. He ran to Fagin's as fast as his legs could go. When he told Fagin what he heard down at the river, Fagin had a fit. He was so angry, he put his hand through a wall. "We'll all hang now!" he shouted.

The next morning Bill Sikes was feeling much better. He got dressed and headed to Fagin's place. There, Fagin and Noah told him what had happened on the bridge. Bill's face turned an angry red. There was fire in his eyes as he ran for the door. Fagin tried to stop him. He knew that Bill was going after Nancy.

When Bill got home, he shouted for Nancy. But she didn't answer. He found her asleep in her bed. He grabbed her covers and pulled them off the bed. "*GET UP!*" he shouted. "*GET UP RIGHT NOW!*"

Nancy could tell from the sound of his voice that she was in big trouble. "Why, Bill," she said, trying not to look frightened, "why are you shouting at me? And why are you looking at me like that?"

Bill was getting madder by the minute. "Stop playing your silly games!" he shouted. "You were followed last night. And every word

you said was heard!"

Nancy's legs began to shake. She knew she had been caught. Her heart raced. Her thoughts raced. There was nothing she could say to save herself.

"Oh, please, Bill," she cried. "Spare my life," she begged. "I have always loved you. Please don't hurt me."

But Bill would not listen. He pulled Nancy by her arm and dragged her out of bed. He dragged her across the room. He put one hand over her mouth and his other hand reached for his gun. Just then, he remembered that the gun would make too much noise. So he took his gun and struck Nancy over the head. He struck her again and again. Blood began to run down her face and into her eyes.

"Please, Bill," cried Nancy, "please don't kill me."

But Bill was so angry that he could no longer hear her. He struck her over and over until she fell dead.

When he saw that Nancy was no longer moving, he became very frightened.

Where can I drag this body? he thought. *If I try to get rid of it, someone is sure to see me. I've got to get out of here!*

Bill washed the blood off himself, then cut the blood spots out of his clothes. He left the house, slamming the door behind him. He ran and ran, going this way and that way. Everywhere he went, shadows seemed to follow him. In his mind he kept seeing Nancy's dead body. But he had nowhere to hide, and so he headed back home.

When Bill got home, Charley Bates was there. "I called the police," said Charley. "You murdered poor Nancy."

Bill had no time to spare. He grabbed a rope and headed out the door. He ran to the roof. He had planned to swing down to the river by a rope. But the rope caught him around the neck. He hanged until he was dead.

Nancy's Murder

COMPREHENSION CHECK

Choose the best answer.

1. First, Nancy walked to London Bridge. Then, just past midnight, Rose and Mr. Brownlow appeared on the bridge. Next,
   ____a. Noah ran home to tell Fagin about the meeting.
   ____b. Noah hid himself down by the river.
   ____c. Mr. Brownlow gave Nancy some money.
   ____d. Bill Sikes beat up Nancy.

2. Mr. Brownlow was not sure if Nancy
   ____a. would meet them on the bridge.
   ____b. could be trusted.
   ____c. was followed.
   ____d. loved Bill.

3. At the river, Nancy told Mr. Brownlow and Rose
   ____a. all about herself.
   ____b. that she needed some money.
   ____c. what Fagin looked like.
   ____d. what she knew about Monks.

4. Monks had a big, red spot on his
   ____a. hand.
   ____b. leg.
   ____c. neck.
   ____d. face.

5. Nancy said
   ____a. she would never leave Bill.
   ____b. she wanted to see Bill hanged.
   ____c. she wanted to leave the country.
   ____d. that she and Bill loved each other.

6. When did Bill Sikes find out about the meeting on the bridge?
   ____a. When Nancy returned home
   ____b. A little after midnight
   ____c. About a week later
   ____d. The next day

7. How did Bill Sikes kill Nancy?
   ____a. He struck her over and over with his gun.
   ____b. He shot her.
   ____c. He put his hand over her face until she stopped breathing.
   ____d. He put a rope around her neck and hanged her.

8. After he killed Nancy, Bill ran from the house. When he returned home, who was waiting there?
   ____a. Monks
   ____b. Fagin
   ____c. Charley Bates
   ____d. Mr. Brownlow

9. Another name for this story could be
   ____a. "Nancy Saves Herself."
   ____b. "All In a Day's Work."
   ____c. "Down By the River."
   ____d. "The End of Bill Sikes."

10. This story is mainly about
    ____a. a young woman who lost her life trying to help another.
    ____b. how Bill Sikes hanged himself.
    ____c. how little Oliver caused so much trouble.
    ____d. a secret meeting on London Bridge.

Check your answers with the key on page 67.

NANCY'S MURDER

VOCABULARY CHECK

drag	hid	often	spare	spot	struck

I. Sentences to Finish
Fill in the blank in each sentence with the correct key word from the box above.

1. I watched Bill _____ the heavy chair across the room.

2. When the car _____ a tree, I heard a loud crash.

3. "How did you get that _____ on your new dress?" asked Mother.

4. Joey _____ his money where no one would find it.

5. My friend asked if I could _____ some money until Friday.

6. I go swimming _____ during the summer.

II. Making Sense of Sentences
Put a check next to YES if the sentence makes sense. Put a check next to NO if the sentence does not make sense.

1. I watched Conrad **drag** the book back to the library. ___YES ___NO

2. Amy **hid** her new dress where her sister could find it. ___YES ___NO

3. Mom goes shopping **often.** ___YES ___NO

4. Gary **struck** the man with his voice. ___YES ___NO

5. The poor man asked if I could **spare** some change. ___YES ___NO

6. The **spot** on my new shirt will not come out. ___YES ___NO

Check your answers with the key on page 71.

This page may be reproduced for classroom use.

BEGINNINGS AND ENDINGS

PREPARATION

Key Words

alike	(ə līk´)	much the same *The two girls looked alike.*
America	(ə mer´ə kə)	the United States *In America, there are 50 states.*
child	(chīld)	a baby; a young boy or girl *Josh was only a child when he came to America.*
daughter	(dô´ tər)	a parent's female child *My son and daughter will come with me on the trip.*
earn	(ėrn)	get in return for work or service *I must earn more money if I am to buy a new car.*
history	(his´ tə rē)	a known past; what was known to have happened 1. *Rob has a history of getting into trouble.* 2. *Let me tell you the history of this old house.*

Beginnings and Endings

Necessary Words

adopt (ə dopt´) to take as one's own
The family will <u>adopt</u> another child.

forgiven (fər giv´ ən) to give up the wish to punish someone
Linda was <u>forgiven</u> for the wrong she had done.

minister (min´ is tər) a servant of God who serves the church
*The <u>minister</u> visited my sick grandmother
yesterday.*

mistake (mis tāk´) to do something wrong by accident; error
Everyone makes a <u>mistake</u> once in a while.

prison (priz´ n) a place where one is shut up against his will for
doing something wrong
The man went to <u>prison</u> for stealing a car.

Beginnings and Endings

The police take Charley to the station house.

Preview: 1. Read the name of the story.
2. Look at the picture.
3. Read the sentence under the picture.
4. Read the first three paragraphs of the story.
5. Then answer the following question.

You learned from your preview that Charley Bates
____a. was a cry-baby.
____b. killed Nancy and Bill.
____c. told the police everything he knew.
____d. lied to the police.

Turn to the Comprehension Check on page 64 for the right answer.

Now read the story.

Read to find out about Oliver's real family.

Beginnings and Endings

When the police got to Bill's, Charley Bates was crying. Nancy and Bill were both dead. "I never thought it would come to this," Charley told the police.

"You had better tell us all you know," said one of the policemen, "or you'll find your own neck around the end of a rope."

Charley told them everything. He told them all he knew about Fagin's history. He told them the little he knew of Monks's history. When he finished his story, the police took Charley to the station house.

Meanwhile, Monks stood in Mr. Brownlow's library. He had been brought there against his will. Mr. Brownlow had a story of his own to tell.

"Monks," he began, "I was a very close friend of Edwin Leeford."

At the sound of that name, Monks's eyes grew big with surprise.

Mr. Brownlow went right on talking. "I know that your name is not really Monks. Your name is Edward Leeford. And you are Edwin's son.

"Your mother and father were married at a very young age. They did not get along with each other. They were not alike in any way. And so, after you were born, your mother and father each went their own way.

"In time, your father fell in love with Agnes, Oliver's mother. But before they could marry, your father became sick. Before he died, he had made a new will. He was leaving most of his money to Agnes and the child she was soon to have.

"When your mother found out about the new will, she became very angry. She felt that *she* should get most of Edwin's money...not Agnes. She went to your father's house one day when he was out. When she found the new will, she burned it. But she left the old will in its place. The old will said that she and her

child, you, would get all the money."

Mr. Brownlow pointed to the picture that hung over the fireplace. "Your father painted that picture of Agnes. He gave it to me. See how much she and Oliver look alike? She was a wonderful woman, Edward. And Oliver is as good as his mother was."

Monks made a terrible face. "I've never forgiven my father for having a child with another woman. And I'll never forgive Oliver for being born."

"Well," said Mr. Brownlow, "I like Oliver very much. And I plan to adopt him."

A few days later Oliver was back at the workhouse where he had been born. All his friends were there. Monks and the Bumbles were there, too. They had been brought there against their will. Mr. Brownlow said it was time to tell the truth...or go to prison with Fagin.

Oliver learned about his father's will. The will said if Agnes had a girl, she would get her part of the money. But if the child were a boy, he would get his money only if he lived a good life. If the boy went bad, the money would go to Monks. That's why Fagin was teaching Oliver to steal. If Oliver got caught and went to jail, Monks would get everything. As for Fagin, Monks would pay him a nice reward.

Mrs. Bumble was in trouble, too. She had sold the locket that should have gone to little Oliver. The workhouse didn't want her working there any more.

"There must be some mistake," said Mrs. Bumble. "I bought that locket! I didn't do anything wrong!"

"In the eyes of the law, you were not wrong," said Mr. Brownlow. "But in your heart you kept Oliver from knowing the truth about his mother."

Mr. Brownlow saved the biggest

surprise for last. "You see, Agnes' father had two daughters. Agnes was the oldest child. When she ran off with Edwin, her father took his other daughter to a strange land. There, he became sick. He died in that strange land without any papers that told who he was. No one knew who would take care of his young daughter.

"Well, it just so happened that Mrs. Maylie had been visiting that strange land. When she learned of the child's poor luck, she took the child in. She brought the child back home with her. And she's been with her ever since."

"*YOU MEAN ROSE IS MY AUNT?*" shouted Oliver, with surprise.

"Yes, Oliver," said Mr. Brownlow. "She is your mother's sister. You really do belong to someone."

A few days later, Harry Maylie had a surprise of his own. "I'm going to become a minister," he told Rose. "I've given up my plans to become rich and famous. If you marry me, Rose, that will make me rich."

The next summer, Rose and Harry got married. Mrs. Maylie went to live with them. And Mr. Brownlow adopted Oliver as his son.

Monks took the little money his father had left him and went to America. But the money and America did not change his bad ways. He was caught stealing and was sent to prison, where he died.

Charley Bates and Noah Claypole changed their lives. With Fagin in prison, they went to work to earn a living. They learned that the best way to stay out of prison was to earn their own money.

And little Oliver's troubles were over for good. The rest of his days were filled with sunshine and laughter. For he finally had the family he had always been looking for.

BEGINNINGS AND ENDINGS

COMPREHENSION CHECK

Choose the best answer.

1. If Charley had not told the police what he knew,
_____a. he would have been charged with the murders.
_____b. Nancy might still be alive.
_____c. Bill might still be alive.
_____d. Bill's neighbors might have killed him.

2. Monks's real name was
_____a. Edward.
_____b. Edwin.
_____c. Ebert.
_____d. Evan.

3. Mr. Brownlow had been a good friend of Monks's
_____a. sister.
_____b. mother.
_____c. father.
_____d. brother.

4. Monks's mother and father
_____a. wanted nothing to do with their son.
_____b. never married.
_____c. did not stay married to each other.
_____d. stayed together to bring up their son.

5. Monks's father, Edwin, had fallen in love with Agnes. But before they married,
_____a. little Oliver was born.
_____b. Edwin died.
_____c. Agnes died.
_____d. Agnes' baby had died.

6. Edwin's *old* will left everything to
_____a. Agnes.
_____b. Agnes and her sister.
_____c. Mr. Brownlow.
_____d. his first wife, and their child, Edward.

7. Edwin's *new* will left everything to Agnes and her child. If the child was a boy, he would get his part of the money if he was a good boy. If he turned bad, the boy's money would go to
_____a. his son Edward.
_____b. his first wife.
_____c. Mr. Brownlow.
_____d. the workhouse, to help the boys there.

8. Monks had spent most of his life trying to
_____a. help his half-brother.
_____b. get his brother's money.
_____c. keep out of jail.
_____d. find Agnes' locket.

9. Another name for this story could be
_____a. "Fagin Goes to Prison."
_____b. "Oliver Finds His Family."
_____c. "Rose and Harry Get Married."
_____d. "Back at the Workhouse."

10. This story is mainly about
_____a. a boy who finds his brother.
_____b. why Fagin went to prison.
_____c. a young boy who found his family.
_____d. how Monks had died.

Check your answers with the key on page 67.

BEGINNINGS AND ENDINGS

VOCABULARY CHECK

alike	America	child	daughter	earn	history

I. Sentences to Finish
Fill in the blank in each sentence with the correct key word from the box above.

1. Jack had a _____ of stealing cars.

2. A young _____ should never cross the street alone.

3. My father came to _____ when he was a young boy.

4. Dad works hard to _____ money for our family.

5. My two friends look _____; I can't tell one from the other.

6. My aunt's _____ is my first cousin.

II. Making Sense of Sentences
Put a check next to YES if the sentence makes sense. Put a check next to NO if the sentence does not make sense.

1. Amy had a **history** of doing good things for others. ___YES ___NO

2. To **earn** some money, you must work for it. ___YES ___NO

3. A **daughter** is a man's first son. ___YES ___NO

4. If two cats look **alike** they look different from one another. ___YES ___NO

5. A young **child** is old enough to drive a car. ___YES ___NO

6. **America** is a free country. ___YES ___NO

Check your answers with the key on page 72.

NOTES

COMPREHENSION CHECK ANSWER KEY
Lessons CTR C-71 to CTR C-80

LESSON NUMBER	QUESTION NUMBER										PAGE NUMBER
	1	2	3	4	5	6	7	8	9	10	
CTRC-71	d	b	a	b	c	b	d	c	b	b	10
CTRC-72	c	d	c	a	b	a	d	a	a	a	16
CTRC-73	b	a	a	d	c	b	c	b	b	c	22
CTRC-74	b	d	c	d	a	b	b	a	a	c	28
CTRC-75	d	c	b	a	b	c	a	c	a	b	34
CTRC-76	d	b	c	d	c	d	a	a	c	a	40
CTRC-77	c	b	d	a	c	a	b	d	b	a	46
CTRC-78	a	d	b	d	c	a	a	d	a	b	52
CTRC-79	b	b	d	c	a	d	a	c	d	a	58
CTRC-80	a	a	c	c	b	d	a	b	b	c	64

○ = Inference (not said straight out, but you know from what is said)

◇ = Sequence (recalling order of events in the story)

△ = Another name for the story

▢ = Main idea of the story

67

NOTES

VOCABULARY CHECK ANSWER KEY
Lessons CTR C-71 to CTR C-80

LESSON
NUMBER

PAGE
NUMBER

71   YOUNG OLIVER   11

I. 1. doctor
2. pleasant
3. spoon
4. astonish
5. sweep
6. bowl

II.

```
P L E I P L A Y A
A B O W L O W A S
S W S W E E P S T
T O P D A W B T O
O O L O S P O O N
N A E C A A W N S
S Y A O N S X I W
W D O C T O R S E
E B P L E A S H P
```

72   OLIVER RUNS AWAY   17

I. 1. age
2. paid
3. lazy
4. downstairs
5. beg
6. cellar

II. 1. c
2. d
3. e
4. b
5. f
6. a

73   FAGIN'S GAME   23

I. 1. judge
2. sparkle
3. thief
4. half, half
5. dirt
6. several

II. 1. NO
2. NO
3. YES
4. NO
5. NO
6. YES

VOCABULARY CHECK ANSWER KEY
Lessons CTR C-71 to CTR C-80

74   **MORE TROUBLE FOR OLIVER**   **29**

I. 1. pillow   *II.* 1. d
      2. tight   2. f
      3. healthy   3. b
      4. laid   4. e
      5. Wipe   5. c
      6. brush   6. a

75   **THE ROBBERY**   **35**

I. 1. we're
      2. against
      3. rich
      4. planned
      5. lying
      6. husband

76   **A CHANGE FOR OLIVER**   **41**

I. 1. disappoint   *II.*
      2. company
      3. doesn't
      4. shadow
      5. beyond
      6. depend

```
D I S A P P O I N T
C X H B E Y C S D E
O W A I D A H S B B
M E D O E S N T E B
P C O M P A N Y Y A
D O W C E T O X O D
I U C O N N O C S I
S H A D D A P P H S
```

VOCABULARY CHECK ANSWER KEY
Lessons CTR C-71 to CTR C-80

77   THE LOCKET   **47**

I. 1. flow
2. became
3. mind
4. become
5. famous
6. below

78   MORE SECRETS   **53**

I. 1. though   *II.* 1. a
2. hug   2. c
3. helping   3. e
4. meet   4. f
5. eleven   5. d
6. steal   6. b

79   NANCY'S MURDER   **59**

I. 1. drag   *II.* 1. NO
2. struck   2. NO
3. spot   3. YES
4. hid   4. NO
5. spare   5. YES
6. often   6. YES

LESSON NUMBER

PAGE NUMBER

80   **BEGINNINGS AND ENDINGS**   **65**

I.
1. history
2. child
3. America
4. earn
5. alike
6. daughter

II.
1. YES
2. YES
3. NO
4. NO
5. NO
6. YES